Wildlife Watching

Butterfly Watching

by Diane Bair and Pamela Wright

Consultant:
Gary A. Dunn
Director of Education
Young Entomologists' Society

CAPSTONE BOOKS
an imprint of Capstone Press
Mankato, Minnesota

Capstone Books are published by Capstone Press
P.O. Box 669, 151 Good Counsel Drive, Mankato, MN 56002
http://www.capstone-press.com

Library of Congress Cataloging-in-Publication Data
Bair, Diane.
    Butterfly watching/by Diane Bair and Pamela Wright.
    p. cm.—(Wildlife watching)
    Includes bibliographical references (p. 45) and index.
    Summary: Describes the physical characteristics and habits of butterflies and discusses how to go about observing them.
    ISBN 0-7368-0320-3
    1. Butterfly watching—Juvenile literature. [1. Butterfly watching. 2. Butterflies.]
I. Wright, Pamela, 1953– . II. Title. III. Series.
QL544.2.B37 2000
595.78'9—dc21   99-18299
                                                                                                        CIP

Editorial Credits

Carrie Braulick, editor; Steve Christensen, cover designer and illustrator;
    Heidi Schoof, photo researcher

Photo Credits

Bill Beatty, 19, cover inset
Colephoto/John S. Reid, 7; Bill Beatty, 27
David F. Clobes, 14, 16, 21
Gail Shumway/FPG International LLC, cover
Index Stock Imagery/Kjell B. Sandved, 4, 24
James P. Rowan, 11
Larry Tackett/TOM STACK & ASSOCIATES, 34
Photo Network, 30
Robert McCaw, 8, 29, 36, 39, 43 (top)
Root Resources/Don & Pat Valenti, 42 (bottom)
Unicorn Stock Photos/Dede Gilman, 41
Visuals Unlimited, 12; Visuals Unlimited/Kjell B. Sandved, 22, 43 (bottom);
    Tim Peterson, 42 (top)

Table of Contents

Chapter 1

Getting to Know Butterflies

Butterflies have interested people for centuries. The ancient Greeks believed that the human soul left the body in the form of a butterfly. In one American Indian myth, the creator makes butterflies to preserve the colors of spring. The creator gathers bright colors from the sky and the flowers to create butterflies.

Butterflies continue to interest people today. Many people go butterfly watching. Some people are attracted to butterflies' bright colors. Others are interested in the different life stages of butterflies. You may have other reasons to go butterfly watching.

Many people are attracted to butterflies' bright colors.

Butterflies are insects. About 20,000 butterfly species exist in the world. Each type of butterfly is called a species. Nearly 700 butterfly species have ranges that include parts of North America. A range is the geographic region where a plant or animal species naturally lives. Butterflies live everywhere in the world except Antarctica. You may have butterflies in your own backyard.

Life Stages of a Butterfly

All butterflies have four life stages. These are the egg, larval, chrysalis, and adult stages.

Butterflies begin as eggs. The eggs of each butterfly species are different. Butterfly eggs can be smooth or rough. They also can be cone-shaped or round. They can be one of several different colors. For example, butterfly eggs can be green, red, or yellow.

Butterflies often lay their eggs on the leaves of plants. Some butterfly species lay only a few eggs. Other species lay more than 1,000 eggs.

Caterpillars hatch from the eggs. A caterpillar also is called a larva. Caterpillars

Some caterpillars have spines.

are shaped like worms. They have three
pairs of legs at the front of their bodies. They
have five pairs of legs at the back of their
bodies. Caterpillars may be one color or a
mixture of colors. Some caterpillars have
spines. These thorn-like parts project from
caterpillars' bodies.

   Caterpillars eat a large amount of food for
their size. Most caterpillars eat plants. But a
few types of caterpillars eat insects. For

example, harvester caterpillars eat tiny insects called aphids.

The developing butterfly next becomes a chrysalis. A chrysalis is covered by a hard outer shell. This shell may be green or brown. It may be covered with bumps.

You often can find a chrysalis hanging from a branch or clinging to a plant stem. A chrysalis does not eat. It uses food the caterpillar ate to develop. The chrysalis begins to split open when the butterfly is fully developed.

An adult butterfly comes out of the split chrysalis. Adult butterflies use a tube-shaped tongue called a proboscis to drink nectar. Flowering plants

Butterflies develop through the egg, larval, chrysalis (left), and adult butterfly life stages.

produce this sweet liquid. Some adult butterflies also drink juice from fruit.

Most adult butterflies live about two weeks. But some butterfly species that live in warm places can live five years or longer.

A Butterfly's Body

A butterfly has three main body parts. These parts are the head, the thorax, and the abdomen.

On its head, a butterfly has two eyes. It also has two antennas. A butterfly uses these feelers to sense its surroundings.

The thorax is the middle part of a butterfly's body. The thorax is slender and has strong muscles to help a butterfly as it flies. Spiracles are located on the thorax. A butterfly uses these tiny holes to breathe. In addition, three sets of legs and two sets of wings are attached to the thorax.

A butterfly has a forewing and a hindwing on each side of its thorax. Forewings are located near the front of the thorax.

Butterflies have two sets of wings.

Pesticides can poison butterflies.

Hindwings are located near the back of the thorax.

A butterfly's wings have tiny scales. The scales can be many colors. They may create a pattern on a butterfly's wings. Many butterflies have wings with spots of color.

A butterfly's abdomen is at the end of its thorax. A butterfly's stomach is located in the abdomen. The abdomen also has spiracles.

Endangered and Threatened Butterflies

Some butterfly species are endangered. These butterflies are in danger of dying out. Other butterfly species are threatened. These butterflies may soon become endangered.

Nearly 20 endangered butterfly species live in the United States. These butterflies include bay checkerspots, Oregon silverspots, Mitchell's satyrs, and Lange's metalmarks.

Some butterflies are threatened or endangered because people destroy their habitats. Habitats are the natural places and conditions in which animals live. People often remove butterflies' habitats when they clear forests to put up buildings or to harvest wood.

Pesticides also are dangerous for butterflies. Farmers and gardeners sometimes spray these chemicals on their plants to kill harmful insects. But caterpillars and butterflies that eat or drink nectar from these plants may become ill and die.

Some people work to protect butterflies. These people may plant trees and flowers to restore forest areas. They may make butterfly gardens. You also can make a butterfly garden.

Make a Butterfly Garden

1. **Conduct a butterfly survey.** Spend a few sunny days watching the butterflies in your area. Notice the different butterfly species and what types of plants they feed on.

2. **Choose an area for your butterfly garden.** This area should be sunny. It should be protected from wind.

3. **Choose plants for your butterfly garden.** Include larval plants and nectar plants. Butterflies lay eggs on larval plants. Caterpillars also feed on larval plants. Adult butterflies feed on nectar plants. Look in a butterfly gardening book or find butterfly web sites on the Internet. This will help you identify larval and nectar plants for butterflies in your area. Include flowers that bloom in spring, summer, and fall.

4. **Arrange your butterfly garden.** Grow large clumps of nectar plants. Place shorter plants at the edges of your garden. Place taller plants near the middle of your garden. Try to place flowers of one color together.

5. **Provide water for butterflies.** Butterflies often drink water from shallow puddles. You may want to include a bird bath or container filled with water in your garden. Put rocks in your water supply. This provides butterflies with a place to sit. Make sure the tops of the rocks are not under water. Butterflies need to drink without becoming wet.

6. **Leave a few weedy patches at the edges of your garden.** Many of these weeds are larval plants for butterflies.

Chapter 2

Preparing for Your Adventure

Learn about the butterflies in your area before you go butterfly watching. You may want to check out a butterfly field guide from your local library or school. Butterfly field guides show what different butterfly species look like and tell where they live. This book has a short field guide on pages 41 to 43.

When to Go Butterfly Watching

In most places, the best months to see butterflies are May through August. Butterflies usually fly in the northern United States and Canada from March to October. Some butterfly

Check out books about butterflies from a library.

species fly throughout the year in the southern United States.

Different butterfly species appear at different times of the year. For example, mourning cloaks often appear in early spring. Check field guides for the best times to look for certain butterfly species.

Go butterfly watching on calm, sunny days. Butterflies rarely fly in rainy or cold weather.

What to Bring

Close-focusing binoculars are very useful for butterfly watching. This viewing tool makes distant objects appear closer. Close-focusing binoculars will help you observe butterflies from a distance. These binoculars are sold at some nature stores.

You may want to bring a net to catch butterflies. You can observe butterflies in these nets after you catch them. Butterfly nets do not harm butterflies.

You also can bring a camera to take photographs of butterflies. You can use a basic

Use a telephoto lens to take pictures of butterflies.

camera if you go to an indoor butterfly house. You often can get very close to butterflies in these places.

It is best to use a camera with a telephoto lens when you look for butterflies in the wild. These lenses are like binoculars. They make distant objects appear closer. You may want to bring a tripod for your camera. These stands with three legs help keep cameras steady when people take pictures. Your school might loan a camera, telephoto lens, and tripod to you. Some camera shops rent these items.

It may be difficult to take pictures of butterflies in the wild at first. Butterflies are small and move quickly. But you may improve your photography skills as you gain experience.

Other supplies can be useful when you watch butterflies. Bring sunblock on sunny days. Sunblock helps protect your skin from sunburn. Wear clothing that blends in with nearby plants. Butterflies may notice you and fly away if you wear bright colors. You may want to bring a butterfly field guide. You also can bring a notebook, sketch pad, pen, or other recording supplies. Use these items to record information about the butterflies you see.

Handling Butterflies
Butterflies must be handled gently. Rough handling can hurt or kill butterflies.

Butterfly nets can help you catch butterflies.

Move slowly when you try to catch butterflies in nets. Many butterflies fly away if you move quickly toward them. Carefully pick up the butterflies you catch. Grasp butterflies underneath their thorax. Do not grab their wings. This may remove butterflies' scales. Butterflies that lose too many scales cannot fly well. You also may damage important veins in butterflies' forewings. Butterflies with broken veins in their forewings will die. Always

release butterflies when you are finished looking at them.

Do not put butterflies in jars. Butterflies may die if they are trapped in jars too long. Jars can become too hot for butterflies.

Do not handle a butterfly egg or chrysalis. These are very fragile. You will probably kill the developing butterfly if you handle an egg or chrysalis.

Safety

Follow safety rules when you go butterfly watching. Do not enter people's property without their permission. Do not go to unfamiliar places alone. You may become lost. Children should bring an adult with them.

Pay attention to your surroundings when you butterfly watch. Other animals may live in the area. Try not to interfere with these animals' habitats. Do not frighten the animals or step on plants. Take any items you bring with you back home. This helps protect the land against pollution.

Do not handle butterfly eggs.

Chapter 3

Where to Look

You can find butterflies almost anywhere there are flowers, sunshine, and open space. Look in your yard or near your home. You may see butterflies in parks. You can look for butterflies in natural wildlife areas or near fruit trees. You may want to visit places that are open to the public for butterfly watching.

Natural Wildlife Areas

Look for butterflies in natural wildlife areas. These places include fields, prairies, and woods. Many national parks and wildlife refuges have natural wildlife areas. Butterflies feed on many plants in these areas.

You often can find butterflies drinking nectar from flowers.

Look for groups of flowers or trees with blossoms. Some butterflies even feed on animal droppings and dead animals.

On cool mornings, you may see butterflies resting on rocks in the sunshine. Butterflies are cold-blooded. Their body temperatures change with their surroundings. Butterflies must warm their thorax muscles in order to fly.

Fruit Trees and Orchards
Look for butterflies near fruit trees and orchards. You may see butterflies drinking the juice of rotting fruit.

Butterflies often are found on fruit that has not been sprayed with chemicals. Sprayed fruit may keep butterflies away.

Rainstorm and Night Shelters
Butterflies find shelter at night and during rainy weather. Some butterflies seek shelter under large leaves. Some slip inside thick piles of leaves or between rocks. Other butterflies perch on stems of grass or twigs. They hold their heads down and press their wings

Some butterflies drink juice from rotting fruit.

together. Butterflies may die during very hard or long rainstorms.

After a rainfall, you may see butterflies sucking water from wet soil. Look for them near mud puddles. You also may see butterflies near streams or on dirt roads and trails.

Winter Living Places

Some butterflies live in areas with cold winters. Butterflies often spend winters in the egg and larval stages. Butterflies in these stages are difficult to find during winter. A few adult butterfly species enter diapause until spring. This resting period helps butterflies save their energy. You may see butterflies in diapause in hollow trees or under piles of leaves. Do not disturb butterflies in diapause.

Monarch butterflies migrate during winter. They fly to overwintering sites when the weather becomes cold. They live at these places until the weather becomes warm again. Monarch butterflies migrate thousands of miles

Butterflies sometimes suck water from wet soil.

across North America. You may see monarchs as they fly. You also may see them resting in trees or bushes.

Look for monarchs at their overwintering sites. Monarchs that live east of the Rocky Mountains migrate to forests in the mountains of Mexico. Monarchs from the western United States and British Columbia, Canada, gather in trees along California's coast.

Public Viewing Areas

Some places are well-known for butterfly watching. These places may have many different butterfly species. They may have butterflies in all four life stages. Many of these viewing places are located in the United States and Canada.

You can visit some butterfly viewing places year-round. These places may have indoor butterfly gardens. But butterfly watching at other places is best only during certain months. For example, you may see monarchs at their overwintering sites only during winter months.

Monarchs gather in large groups at their overwintering sites.

Places to See Butterflies

1 **Natural Bridges State Park, Santa Cruz, California:**
About 150,000 monarchs live here each winter.

2 **Pismo State Beach, Oceano, California:**
Thousands of monarchs gather on eucalyptus trees at North Beach campground from November to March.

3 **Bentsen-Rio Grande Valley State Park, Mission, Texas:**
Many different butterfly species live here from May through November. More than 70 different species have been recorded.

4 **Point Pelee National Park, Leamington, Ontario, Canada:**
More than 85 species of butterflies can be viewed here. Butterfly watching is best at the end of September. Visitors may visit the park during Butterfly Daze. This week features butterfly events.

5 **Butterfly World, Coconut Creek, Florida:**
Butterfly World has the largest butterfly house in the United States. This area has 100 to 150 butterfly species from different countries around the world. Visitors also may see large numbers of Florida's native butterflies.

6 **Victoria Butterfly Gardens, Victoria, British Columbia, Canada:**
More than 30 species of butterflies can be viewed in this indoor butterfly garden.

7 **Cape May Point State Park, Cape May Point, New Jersey:**
This park is an excellent place to view migrating monarchs during late summer. The monarchs usually arrive here in mid-August.

8 **McKee-Beshers Wildlife Management Area, near Gaithersburg, Maryland:**
More than 81 butterfly species live in this area's many habitats. Butterflies can be found near woodland areas, swamps, meadows, fields, and hillsides.

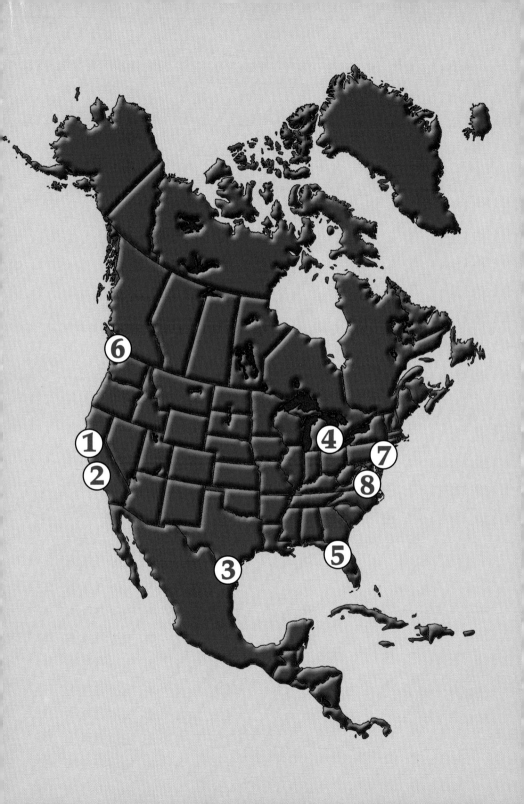

Chapter 4

Making Observations

Different butterfly species have different features. They may have different colors or markings. These features can help you identify each species.

Coloring

Butterflies can be almost any color. For example, they can be red, green, purple, or blue. Most butterflies are a mixture of colors.

Some butterflies have camouflage coloring. Butterflies with these colors blend into their surroundings. These butterflies may match

Most butterflies are a mixture of several different colors.

plants they rest on. Camouflage coloring helps protect butterflies from predators. Predators live by hunting other animals for food. Butterfly predators include lizards and birds.

A caterpillar or chrysalis also may have camouflage coloring. They may look like leaves, seeds, pods, or bird droppings.

Markings

Butterflies can have many different markings. Some butterflies have eyespots. These patterns of scales on butterflies' wings look like eyes. Some types of butterflies have several eyespots. Others have small spots, checks, or bands of color on their wings.

Some butterflies have names that describe their markings. For example, veined white butterflies are mostly white. They have scales along their wing veins. Dotted checkerspot butterflies have a row of white spots along the outer edge of their hindwings. Silver-spotted skippers have a shiny silver band on the underside of their hindwings.

Some butterflies have camouflage coloring.

Sizes

Butterfly sizes vary greatly. Many smaller butterflies such as mormon metalmarks and common checkered skippers have wingspans of less than 1 inch (2.5 centimeters). Wingspan is the distance between the tips of a butterfly's wings. Other butterflies are large. Giant and tiger swallowtails may have wingspans of 5.5 inches (14 centimeters).

Different butterfly species sometimes have similar colors and markings. You then can compare their sizes to tell them apart. For example, gulf fritillary butterflies and pearl crescent butterflies are both orange with black markings. But gulf fritillaries are larger than pearl crescents. Pearl crescents have wingspans of about 1 to 2 inches (2.5 to 5 centimeters). Gulf fritillaries have wingspans of about 2.5 to 4 inches (6.3 to 10 centimeters).

Mimics

Some butterflies are poisonous. Birds and other butterfly predators that eat poisonous butterflies become sick. Predators then avoid poisonous butterflies after they have eaten one.

Viceroys look almost exactly like monarchs.

Mimic butterflies look almost exactly like poisonous butterflies. This helps protect mimic butterflies from predators. For example, viceroy butterflies look almost exactly like monarchs. Monarchs are poisonous to predators. Predators avoid both viceroys and monarchs because they look alike. You may need to look very closely or use a field guide to tell mimics apart from other butterflies.

Butterflies and Moths

Butterflies and moths also look similar. Both are in a group called Lepidoptera.

You can tell butterflies from moths in several ways. Butterflies fly during the day. But most moths fly at night. Butterflies have knobs at the end of their antennas. Moths do not have these knobs. A moth attaches its cocoon to a flat surface. A cocoon is similar to a chrysalis. But a butterfly hangs its chrysalis from a branch or plant stem.

Recording Your Observations

You may want to record your observations about butterflies in a notebook. Note the date and the time of day you see butterflies. Note butterflies' behaviors.

You may make drawings or take photographs of the butterflies you see. You can fill in the drawings with markers or colored pencils.

You may make different observations each time you watch butterflies. Recording your information will help you remember and keep track of your adventures.

Cabbage White

Description: Cabbage whites are the most numerous butterflies in North America. Cabbage whites are mostly white with dark gray wing tips. Males have one black spot on each forewing. Females have two black spots on each forewing. Cabbage whites have a wingspan of about 1 to 2 inches (2.5 to 5 centimeters). Cabbage whites are one of the first butterflies to appear in spring. Adults often fly in small groups. They spend winters as a chrysalis. Females lay single eggs. Cabbage white caterpillars are green. Mature caterpillars have a pale yellow line on their backs. Cabbage white caterpillars sometimes damage crops.

Habitat: Fields, gardens, weedy areas, meadows, roadsides

Food: *Adults:* variety of flowers
Caterpillars: mustard, cabbage, broccoli, cauliflower, and radish plants

■ = Range

Monarch

Description: Monarchs are orange with black veins and borders. The borders are covered with white dots. Monarchs are large. They have a wingspan of about 3 to 5 inches (7.6 to 13 centimeters). Monarchs migrate south to overwintering sites in California and Mexico. They begin flying north again in spring. Monarchs lay eggs as they fly north. Their offspring then finish the northern trip. Monarch caterpillars have yellow, black, and white stripes.

Habitat: Open fields, meadows, prairies, marshes, roadsides

Food: *Adults:* nectar of milkweed plants, variety of flowers
    Caterpillars: milkweed plants

= **Range**

Painted Lady

Description: Painted ladies are orange with black markings. Their forewings have black tips with white spots. They have wingspans of about 2 inches (5 centimeters). Painted ladies have the most widespread range of any butterfly in the world. They are found on every continent except Antarctica. Most adult painted ladies migrate. Painted lady caterpillars are green with black spots. These caterpillars also have spines. Painted lady caterpillars make silk nests on leaves.

Habitat: Fields, meadows, woodlands, gardens, near streams

Food: *Adults:* variety of flowers, often thistles
    Caterpillars: thistles

= **Range**

Tiger Swallowtail

Description: Tiger swallowtails are yellow with black stripes. Their hindwings have blue patches and orange eyespots. They have a wingspan of about 3 to 6 inches (7.6 to 15 centimeters). Two types of tiger swallowtails exist. These are eastern and western tiger swallowtails. Eastern tiger swallowtails mainly live east of the Rocky Mountains. Female eastern tiger swallowtails may be dark brown. Western tiger swallowtails mainly live west of the Rocky Mountains. Tiger swallowtail caterpillars are green.

Habitat: Woodland edges, parks, meadows, river valleys, gardens, weedy areas, near homes

Food: *Adults:* variety of flowers
Caterpillars: tree leaves, mustard plants

= Range

Mourning Cloak

Description: Mourning cloaks are red-purple. Their wing edges have a row of blue marks and yellow borders. They have wingspans of about 3 inches (7.6 centimeters). Mourning cloaks lay their eggs in groups around twigs. Mourning cloaks live long compared to other North American butterflies. Many live nearly a year. Adult mourning cloaks usually hibernate. Mourning cloak caterpillars are red and black with spines. They also are called spiny-elm caterpillars.

Habitat: Edges of woodlands, gardens, parks, near streams

Food: *Adults:* tree sap, rotting fruit, variety of flowers
Caterpillars: tree leaves; often willow, elm, aspen, or cottonwood leaves

= Range

Words to Know

camouflage (KAM-uh-flahzh)—coloring that makes a butterfly look like its surroundings

chrysalis (KRISS-uh-liss)—the third life stage of a butterfly

habitat (HAB-uh-tat)—the natural places and conditions in which an animal lives

larva (LAR-vuh)—the worm-like stage of a butterfly's life; a larva sometimes is called a caterpillar.

migrate (MYE-grate)—to move from one area to another as the seasons change

nectar (NEK-tur)—the sweet liquid in flowers

proboscis (pro-BOS-kiss)—a tongue shaped like a tube; a butterfly uses its proboscis to drink liquid.

range (RAYNJ)—geographic region where a plant or animal species naturally lives

scale (SKALE)—a small, thin plate on a butterfly's wing

To Learn More

Boring, Mel. *Caterpillars, Bugs, and Butterflies.* Young Naturalist Field Guides. Milwaukee: Gareth Stevens, 1998.

Emmel, Thomas C. *Butterfly Gardening: Creating a Butterfly Haven in Your Garden.* New York: Friedman/Fairfax Publishers, 1997.

Hamilton, Kersten. *The Butterfly Book: A Kid's Guide to Attracting, Raising, and Keeping Butterflies.* Santa Fe, N.M.: John Muir Publications, 1997.

Pascoe, Elaine. *Butterflies and Moths.* Nature Close-up. Woodbridge, Conn.: Blackbirch Press, 1997.

Useful Addresses

Canadian Wildlife Service
Environment Canada
351 St. Joseph Boulevard
Hull, QC K1A 0H3
Canada

National Wildlife Federation
8925 Leesburg Pike
Vienna, VA 22184

North American Butterfly Association
4 Delaware Road
Morristown, NJ 07960

Young Entomologists' Society
6907 West Grand River Avenue
Lansing, MI 48906

Internet Sites

Butterfly Zone
http://www.butterflies.com

Children's Butterfly Site
http://www.mesc.usgs.gov/butterfly/butterfly.html

Monarch Watch
http://www.MonarchWatch.org

North American Butterfly Association
http://www.naba.org

Young Entomologists' Society
http://members.aol.com/YESbugs/bugclub.html

Index